FROM HOLY WEEK TO EASTER

Following the God who is going before

GEORGE PATTISON

GW00503778

SLG Press
Convent of the Incarnation Fairacres
Parker Street Oxford OX4 1TB England

www.slgpress.co.uk

FROM HOLY WEEK TO EASTER

Following the God who is going before

© GEORGE PATTISON, 2010

Cover illustration:

'The Women at the Tomb', reproduced by kind permission
of the Provost and Fellows of King's College, Cambridge © 2009

ISBN   978-0-7283-0179-5
ISSN   0307-1405

Printed by:
Will Print   Oxford   England

CONTENTS

iii

INTRODUCTION

THIS SMALL BOOK has developed out of a series of sermons and addresses given in Christ Church Cathedral, Oxford, between Palm Sunday and Good Friday 2007. For reasons that will, I hope, be obvious, I have added a sermon preached at St Helen's Church, Abingdon on the Second Sunday after Easter 2007. I have also added two further meditations: on the mirror of nature and on betrayal. Putting these together provides a text for each day of Holy Week, from Palm Sunday to Easter Day.

The talks are not essentially structured chronologically and do not set out to deal with the events they discuss in a strictly serial way. Rather, they are an attempt to trace the descending path of an ever-deepening spiral, taking us from the very public happenings of Palm Sunday to the utter intimacy of the death and burial. Each step is, in a way, implicit in the one before. Then, in the last sermon, that dark spiral is screwed more tightly still, screwed to bursting-point, tightened till it explodes—and we are thrown back into the world to witness to what we have seen and heard. It is the movement from the hope and expectation generated by Jesus's arrival in Jerusalem to the real fulfilment of that hope on Easter Day, a fulfilment that passes through the annihilation of the children's Hosannahs in the dark night of Holy Week.

This is a movement or pattern that repeats itself continually and in many forms in the religious life: retreat and mission, repentance and forgiveness, sin and salvation, death and resurrection, incarnation and ascension—but it is in the events of Holy Week that this movement finds its most condensed and forceful expression. As the story of this movement, and as the original enactment of this pattern, the Passion narrative becomes a paradigm of religious existence and, in practice if not in theory, more powerfully normative in Christian life than even the Creeds.

Christ Church Cathedral is, of course, a church strongly associated with the milieu of Oxford University, and I am a teaching and researching member of that University. I would, therefore, be hesitant to describe the materials presented here as 'popular', but I do hope that they are not 'academic' in any narrow sense. Some years ago a prominent radical theologian suggested to me that it was becoming impossible to be theologically honest and still to preach in the Church of England. Clearly, the very fact of these sermons implies that I disagree. They are not academic, but they are informed by a wide range of theological study and research. At the same time, they are not written to address or to solve problems in academic theology. They are rooted in the human and spiritual reality of our encounter with those eight days that changed the world, and are not focussed on the theoretical or historical questions that might legitimately be asked about the gospel record. And whilst one might argue that the academic and the human should not ultimately be separated, it is inevitable that, in any given work, one or other aspect is going to be more to the fore. So it is here. Yet, at the same time, I would hope that anyone who has also read my scholarly books would be able to recognize a certain continuity.

As indicated above, all but two of these meditations were delivered as sermons or addresses in the context of liturgy. They were not produced to be published or read. There are, therefore, leaps and omissions in argument that might need to be addressed in a purely written text, and a case could be made for a wholesale rewriting of the material to make it more book-like in this respect. However, I think that it is better if the reader generously undertakes the work of imaginatively reading these words *as if* they were being spoken, allowing me and allowing himself or herself to take advantage of the kind of freedoms that speech especially enjoys. For I am not attempting to instruct, to define, or to exhort, but simply to invite the reader to a closer reflection on his or her own involvement with the story of Holy Week, to look within, and to discover those dimensions of our contemporary psyche that still resonate to the echo of that far-off—yet surprisingly and sometimes frighteningly near—divine event.

GEORGE PATTISON
Christ Church, Oxford, 2009

1.

PALM SUNDAY

'Hosanna!'[1]

THE WHITE CUBE GALLERY, as its name might suggest, is a box-like minimalist building, entirely devoid of external or internal decoration, and dedicated to exhibiting works of contemporary art. Tucked discreetly away in a small courtyard in London's West End, it is not a gallery that aims to reach out to the wider public; it's strictly for those who like that sort of thing and are able to draw breath in that rather stratospheric atmosphere where art and money meet. All in all, it's not a place where you might expect to find significant commentary on the Gospel of one who proclaimed a blessing on the poor and on the poor in spirit.

I went to the White Cube Gallery for the first time just over a fortnight ago to see an exhibition by Anselm Kiefer, a contemporary German artist whose work by no means aims at being popular. Kiefer became famous in the 1970s for massive canvasses painted in blacks and browns, worked with mud, straw, lead, wire and stones, as well as paint; images of landscapes laid waste by war and genocide; work laying bare the moral and material scars of a nation traumatized by all that it had done and all that it had suffered in the dark time of the artist's childhood. Not much to shout 'Hosanna' about there.

How significant this may be as an index of the times in which we live, I do not know, but 'Hosanna' was just what the latest exhibition by this artist—ravaged by the memory of Nazism—displayed for a monied, secular, postmodern audience, was in fact about, for it centred on an installation

---

[1] Matt. 21: 9; Mark 11: 9-10; John 12: 13.

entitled, simply, 'Palm Sunday'. Of course, because this was a work by an artist such as Kiefer, the theme of Palm Sunday was not treated quite as it is treated in church. Entering the clinical, whitewashed, brick and plate-glass environment of the gallery, we were immediately confronted by a massive felled palm tree, its roots still clogged with earth, stripped of its branches and lying diagonally across the gallery floor, like some monstrous archaic corpse. Three of the walls were blank; the fourth was covered floor to ceiling and end to end with two rows of large canvasses, twenty-two in all, worked in a multitude of materials—paint, clay, sand, metal. Many had a palm branch or frond daubed in whitewash and stuck onto the painted background. Most had the words 'Palm Sunday' scrawled on them in the artist's distinctive hand— one in English, one in German, another in French, Russian, Swedish, and so on: Palm Sunday—*Palm Sonntag*—*Verbnoe voskressenie*—a festival for people of every tribe, nation and tongue.

These multilingual inscriptions implied that this was an action, an event, we can understand in any and every language; something that calls to us from a level deeper, larger, beyond the level of language—for where language divides and, Babel-like, confuses, this celebration unites, gathers us up into the noisy crowd of welcomers, and pulls us all along in the wake of the man on the donkey.

But what is this place beyond language from which the festival spirit of Palm Sunday springs? What chord of common humanity does it touch? In a word, I suggest, it is *hope*, or, more precisely, the expectation of hope fulfilled, of a promise kept. A promise kept needs no great commentary— promises and keeping them are things that even pre-school children know about (and it's no wonder their shouting filled the air on that day), and if the children were to be silenced, then, he said, even the stones would cry out. Wherever there is hope in the world, wherever there is belief that life's promise is not in vain, Palm Sunday can be understood—even in the heart of the monied, secular, postmodern world of a West End gallery.

For who, after all, is finally, totally, entirely hopeless? Of course, great suffering, war, persecution, public and private trauma can crush hope, but it is the natural, proper, true state of the human being to be a being of hope; and there is a very real sense in which it can be said, we *are* what we hope for. Even where what we hope for is something fantastic, something impossible, something that never could be fulfilled, having that hope will shape and mould and make us into the very particular person that each of us is. Hope for something impossible—like a kingdom of justice on earth, like a God amongst us as one of us, a brother-God, a friend-God, a donkey-riding God, a child-friendly God—and even if it never comes true, you will be a different person from the one whose hope is for this life only, for what is merely possible, for what good luck or hard work might be expected to deliver.

And how different our public debate about religion would be if we re-conceived it as a debate about hope rather than about belief. Once the question is, 'Do you *believe* in God?', the only real answers are 'Yes' or 'No'—or, if you're an Anglican liberal, 'Maybe'—as if God is some kind of object out there, some kind of fact, some kind of being that might or might not exist. It's as if we all know what we mean by God, and the question is only whether God exists, like Bigfoot[2] or life in space.

Even if we have a rather more sophisticated picture than that, and our God is depicted—let's say, more poetically—with delicate shading and suitably blurred edges, or analysed—let's say, more metaphysically—with crystal-clear

---

[2] Bigfoot is an ape-like creature which is said to inhabit forests, mainly in the Pacific Northwest region of North America.

precision and definition, it still often sounds as if the task is matching up an idea in our minds with an entity out there, somewhere in space or time, or somewhere outside space and time in metaphysical or conceptual space.

But how would it be if we began thinking of God less as something or someone to believe in—something or someone who might or might not exist—than as the best object of our best and truest hopes, the express image of all our human longings for a richer, fuller, more just, truer way of life; as the promise that the best is yet to come, and we can be more than we are and other than we are? How would it be if we began thinking of God not so much as the Alpha, the God who was in the beginning, but as the Omega, the God who is the life of the world to come?

If we reformulated 'the God debate' in this way, then the question would be less, 'Do you believe in God?' than: 'What do you hope for?' 'On what have you set your heart?' 'Is it something you would dare to call *divine*?' 'Is it something worthy of being called "good", "godly", "holy"?' 'Is it something that all—and not just you alone—could call a blessing?' Then there would be much more to say than 'Yes' or 'No', or 'Maybe'. Then we couldn't even begin to talk about religion without laying bare what it is we're really looking for in life. Then we would see much less of the kind of religion in which belief in God makes no tangible difference to the believer's life.

Philosophers have pointed out that it is rather difficult to see how an 'is' can lead to an 'ought', how believing something to be the case tells us what we ought to be doing—but what we hope for immediately communicates something of what we are aiming to do. We all have hopes of some kind or other, and some of them are probably rather disreputable, but when what we hope for is good, it will keep us generously open to, and active in, the world about us. For how can we curl up into the closed circuit of our own private agendas if

4

our veins are throbbing with the sense that life is a promise seeking fulfilment?

Palm Sunday: a moment in time—a spring moment—when that promise seems about to burst the buds of waiting and desire, when the hum of a crowd spreads hope like wildfire, when children and stones cry 'Hosanna!'—a dry run for *that* day when dreams will come true, when sorrow and sighing shall flee away, and we shall be able in spirit and in truth to say: 'Blessed is the One who comes in the day of the Lord'. Even in the monied, secular, postmodern world that 'New Britain' has become, this hope is never without witness. Could we even be human without it?

2.

THE MIRROR OF NATURE

'From the fig-tree learn its lesson.'[3]

JESUS ENTERS the city in triumph, in what we would call the full glare of publicity. His appearance elicits a spontaneous and heartfelt 'Hosanna' from the shouting, swirling crowds. Something about him triggers that readiness for hope that is one of our deepest human traits. But he does not stay in the city. Each night he withdraws to Bethany, escaping the heat and dust of the city for the relative cool and calm of the country. And out there—away from the noise, away from the thronged streets and packed houses, out of sight of the towering buildings that bespeak imperial and royal power or that house the worship of official religion—he takes a step back from the human world that can so easily be 'too much with us, late and soon',[4] and moves a step closer to the traditional world of the countryside, shaped and moulded by the rhythms of nature, and limited by powers and forces not of our human making. This is a movement between city and country with which many of us are familiar on a daily or regular basis. Indeed, it is one of the basic rhythms of our modern world. Nature, the country, 'out there'—this is where we find healing from the stresses and strains of city life, where we find the space to re-connect and the time to get back in touch with ourselves.

Compared with many religious texts, ancient and modern, Eastern and Western, the New Testament says little about human beings' relation to the non-human world, to what we have come to call 'nature'. There is little here to satisfy would-be worshippers of the Great Pan, no sacred

---

[3] Mark 13: 28; Matt. 24: 32.
[4] From a sonnet by William Wordsworth.

6

groves or healing wells. It is true that there are sayings and parables that appeal to the birds of the air and the lilies of the field; the colours of sunset and sunrise become a metaphor for human beings' capacity for reading the will of God; and—not least—Jesus shows himself to be Lord of nature by walking on water and calming the storm with a single word. Yet none of this even approximates to the love of natural beauty or the glimpses of God in natural forms that seem to be found in ancient paganism, or in such religious traditions as those of China, Japan, Druidism, or of the Native Americans. And this is true of biblical religion as a whole. Undoubtedly there were Old Testament writers—such as the great anonymous poet who produced the book of Job—who had a keen sense for the majesty and complexity of the non-human forces and creatures astir beyond the human world. Yet, despite the recognition of God's wisdom manifested in the cycle of the seasons or the sublime beauty of the night sky, the relationship between human beings and their environment is often depicted in a hostile or adversarial way. After Eden, we have to earn our bread by the sweat of our brows, and just being born into the world is possible only in and through the pains of childbirth. God is recognized in nature, but precisely in the way that nature so terrifyingly transcends and crushes our human capacities for understanding and action—as when Job is ordered to marvel at the vast Leviathan and the fearsome crocodile.

Unsurprisingly, this sense of conflict between human beings and their environment is today seen by many as one more counter-argument to the claim that biblical religion can serve the religious needs of contemporary humanity. Surely, we hear it said, the religion we need now is not a religion preaching dominion over nature, but a religion of peaceful co-existence with the environment, a green or eco-theology that the Bible seems rarely capable of supporting.

Nor would this view be encouraged by one of the stories associated with Jesus's rural retreats to Bethany. For it is there—out in the peace and quiet of the country—that we see one of the most bewildering and, some think, one of the most scandalous episodes of the gospel: the cursing of an innocent fig tree. The story is short, and to the point. In the morning, preparing to go back into Jerusalem, Jesus feels hungry and looks for figs on a wayside fig-tree. But it is not the season for figs, and so there is no fruit on the tree. Jesus, it seems, has made a mistake. But instead of acknowledging this, he vindictively turns on the hapless tree and curses it, so that it either withers up at once (according to Matthew[5]), or has withered by the time they return to Bethany (according to Mark[6]). When the disciples are astonished at this display of power, Jesus uses it for a saying—probably rather better known than the story itself—about the power of prayer, that if you have faith, and command even a mountain to be lifted up and thrown into the sea, then it will happen. 'Whatever you ask for in prayer with faith, you will receive', he says.[7] Killing fig trees and tearing down mountains are perfectly acceptable actions for Christians, it seems. But is that really what this puzzling, and gratuitously unpleasant story, is really about?

This is one of those texts about which it might be helpful to turn to biblical scholars, who might tell us that in its present form the story is clearly the result of tradition; that it is a compilation of different sources and sayings which perhaps meant something quite different in their original context. But even as it stands, the story is perhaps susceptible of a more generous interpretation than the obvious one which has just been given.

---

[5] Matt. 21: 19.
[6] Mark 11: 20.
[7] Matt. 21: 22; cf. Mark 11:24.

In the Middle Ages, human beings' relation to nature—or, more precisely, God's relation to human beings as mediated by nature—was often conceived in the figure of a mirror: nature was a mirror in which we could read God's purposes for human life. Each aspect of nature, each of the four elements, each creature, each bird, beast, flower or natural occurrence, had a deep meaning in the divine scheme of things. If we only knew how to look, then we would see God's will for us clearly, if not fully, revealed. (A full revelation would, of course, depend on the additional knowledge of God revealed in scripture, in the lives of the saints, in the sacraments, and in Christ himself.) A red rose represents the choir of martyrs; a white rose, the choir of virgins. Spring is a symbol of baptism; summer of eternal life. 'Every creature is a shadow of truth and life', as Honorius of Autun wrote. This comes as a relief, for whatever the Bible may or may not have said, Christian tradition seems, after all, not to be without some sense for the co-inherence of divine and human in the wonders and beauties of the natural world.

But is this vision of co-inherence a true vision; or, to put it better, is it simply true? The answer is, surely not. If we look back through history; if we look around at human beings' current treatment of their environment; if we look more intimately at our relation to our own human nature; then we do not see an image of harmony perfectly reflected in the shining surface of a clear mirror. It is, at best, an image glimpsed obscurely, 'in a mirror, dimly'.[8] Whether we call it exercising dominion, or however we understand it, we have in fact destroyed thousands of species of our fellow creatures. We have polluted rivers, seas, skies, and field. We have stripped mountains and valleys of their original forests. We have reduced fertile plains to dustbowls; and, most seriously of all, we are in grave danger of turning the whole planet into

---

[8] I Cor. 13: 12.

9

a greenhouse in which we ourselves could be collectively smothered. Nor is the story much better with regard to our own human nature. Such natural appetites as food and sex are clearly necessary to life and are part of our created being. But in an age of ever-increasing obesity and other eating disorders, of pornography, including internet videos of the 'live' sexual abuse of children, we can scarcely claim to be at one with our own human nature. Our natural self-assertion and the territorial imperative we share with other animals seem constantly to overstep their natural limits and drive us into unnatural acts of murderous violence, as the wars, rumours of wars, and daily crimes of our society testify. This is not to say that there may not be individuals here and there who have found a better way. We can concede that there may be much common wisdom about how to do things better, how to be at ease in our bodies, how to cherish and be thankful for our appetites, rather than constantly over-indulging them. But we can scarcely say that humanity as a whole is at peace with nature, external or internal, 'natural' or human. We are somehow dislocated from our world and from ourselves. The values, actions and institutions that make up our man-made world are unavoidable; and yet, tragically, they separate us from our created being, from the world of non-human creatures, and from our own creaturely balance of forces.

And that, I think, is what this story, this acted parable, is telling us. If today we look into the mirror of nature—whether it is upwards to a sky that is now rarely to be seen except as criss-crossed by vapour trails from polluting jet engines, or whether it is inwards to the apparently spontaneous desires engendered in us by a culture of consumption, status, and wealth—we do not see ourselves or our world as we 'naturally' are. We see an image, a hint, a glimpse, a shadow, perhaps. But the truth of that image, the figure behind the shadow, escapes us. To paraphrase Shakespeare, 'we are not what we are'. If Palm Sunday launches us onto a journey of hope and expectation, that strange encounter with the barren fruit tree reminds us that what we hope for is not always good. The truth of who we are, of what we want, of what we should want, of what we might in justice expect; this truth is not just lying there, just waiting to be picked up. It is a truth we must struggle for, and in this struggle we will chiefly have to struggle against ourselves, struggling on behalf of the created 'natural' goodness we dare not claim to see in our lives as they are, here and now, but which is the image—the natural divine image—of what we shall be.

I shall, then, be biblical critic enough to suggest the following: that the meaning of this unnerving encounter with the fig-tree is not so much to be found in the saying about the power of prayer and the power of prayer 'over' nature that follows, but rather in a comment that is found in Jesus's prophetic warnings about the times to come:

> From the fig-tree learn its lesson: as soon as its branch becomes tender and puts forth its leaves, you know that summer is near. So also, when you see these things taking place, you know that he is near, at the very gates.[9]

That is how in 'nature' it should be. For us, as we are now, it is otherwise: we put out our hands to gather figs, but gather thorns. And the meaning is not that we should spurn or ignore the obscure or threatening images that nature today reflects back to us, but that we should start to read them more carefully, to see them more clearly, to respond to their promptings more humbly. For the fig-tree that did not bear fruit when Jesus paused beside it is an image of the city that did not know the hour of its visitation, as well as an image of the person who does not use the opportune time to look again at what they are hoping for and what they are working towards.

---

[9] Mark 13: 28-9.

11

3.

PROPHECY

'Woe to you!'[10]

JESUS ARRIVES in Jerusalem in an atmosphere of festival—party-time for the whole city—heat and dust, children shouting, and if they stopped, even the stones would cry out. But it doesn't last long.

His first stop is the Temple, where he seems to be spoiling for a fight, driving out 'all who were selling and buying in the Temple',[11] overturning tables, and, in some accounts, setting about him with a lash. And it doesn't stop there. The next day he returns to the attack: 'Woe to you, Scribes and Pharisees!'[12] This is prophecy in the tradition of Amos, Jeremiah and Ezekiel, naming and shaming the religious corruption of the Temple and of the public religion of the land.

'Prophecy' is, of course, a word that has remained current in the language of religion from biblical times till now. Many theologians, bishops and clergy tell us that 'prophetic witness' is integral to the Christian message. But once we've got over the misconception that prophecy is something vaguely akin to astrology, deducing the course of future history from the more obscure passages of the Book of Revelation, there are still issues around just what 'prophecy' really is, or should be, in the Church today. No better place to start, we might think, than with the kind of prophetic action and teaching practised by Jesus himself, and nowhere more so than in the days of his arrival in Jerusalem.

---

[10] Matt. 23: 13-39.
[11] Matt. 21: 12.
[12] Matt. 23: 25.

In our contemporary world, prophecy is often understood in political terms, as if the prophetic ministry of the Church is to pronounce judgement on the misdirected policies and programmes that hold sway in the national and international order; or prophecy is also understood in ethical or moral terms, as if the Christian prophet's task was to unmask the norms and niceties of our society and reveal them as the glittering vices they really are.

It goes almost without saying that there is much misconceived and misdirected policy in the affairs of nations, and the result is often misery on a colossal scale. It is also doubtless true that much of what our society applauds as achievement and success is no more than legalized egoism, and far from what is most worthy of human hope. But let us look at the prophetic action and teaching of Jesus in these few days in Jerusalem—since, after all, it remains true that the pupil is not above the teacher, and we should not look to do more in our prophesying than he sought and achieved in his.

There were many policies and programmes, many moral corruptions and perverted values Jesus could have addressed. He could have denounced slavery: he did not. He could have denounced the making of wars: he did not. He could have denounced military occupations: he did not. He could have denounced insurgency: he did not. He could have denounced terrorism—he did not. He could have denounced torture and the brutal repression of terrorism: he did not. He could have denounced the waste of public money on lavish entertainments and prestigious but pointless building projects, when millions went about in poverty: he did not. He could have denounced a culture in which violence was often treated as entertainment: he did not. He could have denounced homosexuals: he did not. He could have denounced the exclusion of homosexuals: he did not. He could have denounced the political order of his country: he did not. He could have denounced the tax-system: he did not. He could have spoken on all these topics that are of such burning interest to us, for they were all well represented in the world in which he lived: but he did not. In fact, it seems he didn't do or say very much in any of the areas that religious leaders today see as the natural focus of prophetic action and teaching. What, then, did he do? What did he say?

Perhaps the key to answering this question is to shift the focus slightly and notice against whom he acted and on whom he pronounced his woes. In each case, his primary target—arguably his sole target—was the religious leadership of Temple and Synagogue. It is the Temple traders, the Sadducees, the Scribes and Pharisees who are the objects of his attack. And why does he attack them? In a word: because of their *hypocrisy*.

The 'crimes' of the religious leaders are spelt out neither in terms of their theological errors, nor in terms of their social consequences. But they are spelt out in terms of their inconsistency in teaching one thing and practising another; in paying tribute to Scripture as the Word of God and the source of religious authority, whilst undermining it by the way they interpret it, putting all their efforts into what is at best of marginal importance in religion, and neglecting what is truly important; in seeing religious practice and virtue as a basis for drawing distinctions between human beings; and in seeing religious worship as an occasion for displays of superiority and privilege.

Many of the particular arguments are, inevitably, of their place and time. Clergy of the Church of England or of any other modern Church are unlikely to be accused of inappropriately tithing 'mint, dill, and cummin'.[13] But the shape of the accusation is easy, only too easy, to apply to the life of the Christian Church in just about every period of its history. For the heart of the matter is simple—stunningly

---

[13] cf. Matt. 23: 23.

simple. It is whether we are truly prepared to give what is God's to God.

The truly religious community is not a community in which some have authority over others, in which there are institutionalized distinctions between teachers and learners, in which religion is simply public performance, liturgy. The truly religious community is a community defined by the fact that its heart, and the hearts of all its members, are set on God and what is God's; set not on being God's representatives, God's people, God's Church, but simply on the love and service of God, with heart, soul, mind. And if, as I suggested in thinking about Palm Sunday, what is most decisive for our God-relation is that we understand this as a relationship of hope, there can be no question of the Church, or of some group, some order, some rank, within the Church, 'having' a superior knowledge or understanding of God or God's mind that would enable them to usurp God's own authority in the Church.

Why not? Because, since it is a matter of hope, all that God will be for us is not yet revealed; even the best of our visions and dreams point only to what is still to come. We all, more or less, see, at best 'in a mirror, dimly',[14] until 'that day'. There is no possession; only waiting, expecting, looking for; and therefore no basis for any to be called rabbi, teacher, father. Hierarchies, orders, offices, should therefore never obscure the reality that there is only one humanity, and if our religion fails to confirm us in a deep sense of being of one blood with all our fellow human beings and even, beyond the human family, with the whole community of creaturely life, then we can be sure that such religion is no longer giving what is God's to God: such religion has become an instrument of division, ambition (petty or great), ego, 'I, me, myself' or 'We, us, people like us'.

---

[14] I Cor. 13: 12.

The prophecy of Jesus is not directed against the failure, the malice, or the corruption of either the Roman or the Herodian State, and if it had been, it would now be no more than historically interesting. As directed almost solely against the religious order of his time, it remains for us a question we must address: What is our religion? What interests, what hope, does it serve? Is it helping us give what is God's to God? Such questions are not posed so much for the sake of criticizing others, bishops or archbishops, synods or summits, but as a mirror that each of us may—each of us must—hold up to ourselves, our hearts, our hopes, if we do not wish to be the people against whom the prophecies and the woes of Holy Week are spoken.

4.

TEACHING

'Day after day I sat in the Temple teaching.'[15]

JESUS'S ARRIVAL in Jerusalem began in a spirit of festival. It soon turned into trouble, as he attacked the Temple traders, made fools of the Sadducees, and pronounced a series of terrifying 'Woes' on the Scribes and Pharisees—'hypocrites', he called them.

But if the atmosphere is at times electric, if the tense exchanges between Jesus and his opponents crackle with anger and the threat of violence, Jesus has another audience for whom he is no longer a prophet but a teacher. He teaches, not by arrogating to himself the privileges, powers and pay-packet of a teacher, but by pointing the audience back to the one thing needful, to the love of God with heart, soul, mind; to the coming time that will reveal all that their hearts have been set upon; to the truth that, since God is God, then all humans are but human and are therefore bound together in one single, indivisible family, in which even the strangers, the failures, and the prisoners, guilty and innocent, stand on the same basic footing.

The first three gospels agree in telling us that, in these days, Jesus came to the Temple and taught, that crowds gathered to hear him; and Luke adds the important qualification that his teaching involved 'telling the good news'. But on first reading, it has to be said that this is not obvious. Whichever of the gospels we turn to, the emphasis seems to be on the coming judgement, the day when the Son of Man will appear, when the sun will be darkened and the moon no longer shine, when the Temple will be levelled to

---

[15] Matt. 26: 55.

the ground, when the disciples will be flogged and persecuted, when the foolish bridesmaids will be locked out of the wedding banquet,[16] when the sheep and the goats will be separated,[17] and the man who failed to use his talent be thrown into the 'outer darkness' where there will be 'weeping and gnashing of teeth',[18] when the bad tenants who refused to pay rent to their Lord and slew his son will be destroyed and their vineyard will be given to others.[19] Judgement Day: rewards for the good, but punishments for the bad; God as cosmic superego; a religion of fear; a recipe for the kind of guilt that drives one person to joyless do-gooding and another to an equally joyless menu of sex, drugs, and rock-and-roll.

But to hear Jesus's teaching in those terms is to mishear it. There can be no denying that the parables he tells in these days have happy endings for some and pretty miserable endings for others, but to apply them in the way I've just sketched is precisely to forget that these are not allegories but parables, not futurology but exhortation. It would have been pointless even to tell such stories, just as it is pointless for us to go on telling them, if it is forgotten that each time the story is told, each listener is free to decide who they want to be in the story and what the story means to them. These stories are not about describing how God's cosmic plan is unfolding according to some necessary but inscrutable logic. Each of these stories presents the hearer with a choice. Each of these stories appeals to our freedom. Each of these stories appeals to our judgement. Each of these stories asks us: 'How—and who—do you want to be?' 'On what have you truly set your heart?' 'Is it really on something that would be worth keeping in some great collective catastrophe?' 'Is it something you

---

[16] Matt. 25: 10-11.
[17] Matt. 25: 32-3.
[18] Matt. 25: 30.
[19] Matt. 21: 41.

would be unashamed to confess before God in that moment when the secrets of all hearts are revealed?'

In meditating on the acted parable of the fig-tree and on Jesus's words of prophecy, I suggested that what is being offered in each case is a kind of mirror that we are invited to hold up to our own hearts; a kind of instrument for self-examination; a way of asking ourselves whether we really love the things of God, whether we really want to give what is God's to God. This invitation is prophetic when (as so often) it reveals a sharp and painful difference between the outside and the inside, between the splendid decoration on the outside of the tomb, and the rotting bones within—a difference Jesus condenses into the repeated charge: 'Hypocrites!'

In these terms, there is no real difference between Jesus's work as a prophet and his work as a teacher. In each case, it is the same mirror, the same challenge, that is held up to each of his listeners; the same question: 'How does what you say you believe relate to what you really want?' But whereas some experience this question as judgement, others experience it as opportunity, invitation, promise. And even those who, on first reading, experience it as judgement; even those who wince at the light these words cast on their own religious lives; even those who recognize themselves in the foolish bridesmaid or the pathetic man with the one talent he insists on hiding; even those who have to concede that they have not always been pro-active in feeding the hungry, giving shelter to the homeless or visiting the prisoners—even all of these can so recognize themselves in the mirror of his word as to find in it an opportunity and an invitation to change.

The great Christian reformer John Calvin once said of his conversion that, 'God subdued my heart to teachableness'— and perhaps this is a clue as to whether we hear Jesus's words as prophecy or as teaching. To discover that what we really want is something rather different from giving to God

19

what is God's—such as, what we really want is to keep something of God's for ourselves: a little bit of his glory, a little bit of his power, a little bit of his wisdom—is to find ourselves being judged. It can become a 'Woe' upon us if we do not regard ourselves as capable of being changed, but rather identify ourselves with the history of how we came to this point of discovery, and say, 'This is how I am; this is who I am; I can be no other.' An example of this is the character in an Ingmar Bergman film who, faced with the truth of his vile behaviour, says of himself that he is like an actor who has only ever played one role, and this role has now taken so strong a grip on him that if he were to throw it away he would cease to exist (he is actually a bishop!). But this is only one way of reacting. We can equally experience such revelations as opportunities to be taught, changed, and transformed, if we let our hearts be subdued to teachableness. The teachable heart is a heart that finds occasion for learning in each new revelation of life, and for the teachable heart, even the realization that it is falling short of the best it could be is a challenge to raise its game; a calling to learn, to become, something new.

Every day, Jesus was teaching in the Temple. Not teaching in the manner of the expert, who has some information or a technique that the learner needs to acquire before he can learn or become proficient. All that this teaching involves is, ultimately, the learner himself or herself. All this teaching asks of us is the question: 'What do you really want?'—not, note, 'What do you say you want?' 'What do you believe you want?' but, 'What do you want?' 'What do you hope for?' And if you don't know how to answer, you don't need any learning resources other than yourself. The meaning of the teaching is simply—your life. What sort of life is it? Is it the sort of life you want it to be? Is it a life you think is worth living? And, if not, will you let your life be made new?

I realize that I'm perhaps making Jesus sound rather like another famous teacher of the ancient world—Socrates. Socrates, too, taught in such a way that learners were led back to themselves, to the intuitive ability each of us has for understanding the truth of geometry and mathematics, but also, Socrates believed, for understanding goodness, truth, and justice. But, as one modern writer has put it, the similarity between Jesus and Socrates consists in their dissimilarity. For Socrates believed that each of us has the capacity to recognize what is good and that, once we have recognized it, we will do it. The only thing holding us back is ignorance. The teaching of Jesus is, in a way, more troubling, more complex. Jesus almost certainly never believed the kind of view we find in some Christian theology, that human beings are incapable of doing good. But he did know that, face to face with what is truly good, we have a choice, and that, at that moment of choice, things can go wrong. We can refuse to choose—Jerusalem can miss the hour of its visitation—or we can make the wrong choices, and the Son of Man will be handed over to be put to death. But what we choose is not something external, not a policy or a programme or a set of values. It is at bottom a choice of ourselves, a matter of deciding who we want to be.

Faced with that choice, that decision, may we be truly teachable. May we learn that choosing ourselves means, finally, choosing God; and choosing God is choosing not judgement but life, or, more accurately, choosing the judgement on ourselves that leads to life.

5.

FRIENDSHIP

'You are my friends.'[20]

IN THE PROPHECY he directed against the Sadducees, Scribes and Pharisees, and in the teaching that he gave to the crowds in the Temple, Jesus held up a mirror to his listeners, a mirror in which they could see the difference between the lives they were living and the promise of the Kingdom of God, and which they variously experienced as judgement and as teaching.

Both prophecy and teaching were very much public events, delivered in the Temple, in front of the crowds, in full hearing of all. The scene to which we now turn our attention is of a very different kind. It is an intimate gathering of a dozen or so men and, probably, some women, who have mostly been together for at least a couple of years; who have shared adventure, adulation, hostility and danger. They have at various times enthused each other, competed with each other, debated with each other, and quarrelled with each other. They know each other pretty well. Many groups could be described in these terms: a military unit, a sports team, a research project, a king and his counsellors, a guru and his disciples, a philosopher and his pupils; and perhaps the little society of Jesus and his disciples is a bit like all of these, but it is also a bit unlike any of them. Early Christian art depicted Jesus wearing a philosopher's pallium and the disciples as enquiring students, while many of our hymns and prayers speak of him as King, Master, Lord, or Captain, and of his ancient and modern disciples as subjects, servants, or soldiers. But if we believe what Jesus did and what he said at the Last Supper he shared with Peter and the others, then he is not a Master or Lord like any other, but himself a servant;

---

[20] John 15: 14.

22

and they are not servants (any more) but friends. Some of you may as children have been read to from the Ladybird children's book *Jesus the Friend*,[21] but the point being made here is not that he is our friend, but that we are, or may become, his friends and, if his friends, then friends of God.

Friendship is one of the great human experiences. Ralph Waldo Emerson said it was 'too good to be believed'[22] and, as a more recent American source than Emerson has it: your friends are there for you, the only ones who know what it's like to be you; the ones with whom you're at your best, even when you're at your worst; as well as the ones you laugh with.

Christians, it has to be said, have sometimes been suspicious of human friendships and have seen in them a potential obstacle in the relation of the self to God. Augustine, who seems to have had a more than usual gift for friendship, nevertheless reproached himself for the tears he wept at the death of a friend. These tears seemed to him to betray a lack of faith in God. Others have been more appreciative: the medieval writer Aelred of Rievaulx rewrote a line from St John to read: 'He that abides in friendship abides in God, and God in him.'

But whatever we might think of friendships with—well— our friends, it's not obvious that 'friendship' is an obvious or natural feature of our relation to God. Surely, the difference between God and human beings is too great for us to be friends. God is in heaven, and human beings are on earth. God is God, and we are but as dust. How could there be friendship between two such unequal beings? Even to think of such a thing seems to betray that old familiar hubris of our wanting to be as gods, our wanting to claim a little bit of what

---

[21] *Stories about Jesus the Friend*, Ladybird Books, series 606A, 1961.
[22] 'Friendship, like the immortality of the soul, is too good to be believed': Ralph Waldo Emerson (1803-82), 'Friendship', *Essays*.

is God's for ourselves. Perhaps that's why so few church buildings allow you to feel that going into God's house is like going to the house of a friend. This is not a home away from home. This is where you are taught to know your place!

Perhaps the worry is that, in the closeness of friendship, we might lose that sense of the Majesty of God, the distance and ineffability of the Godhead that elicits our most sublime feelings of worship and adoration. Yet friendship does not mean that the friend is in every case simply 'another self', someone who likes the same clothes, enjoys the same music, has the same politics, practises the same religion as I do— although there are friendships like that. Many friends, like many marriages, are odd couples, as ill matched as chalk and cheese—and yet sometimes these are the best and strongest friendships. I have been having essentially the same argument about politics with one of my friends for nearly fifty years, and it's a long way from being resolved. Friends aren't, or don't have to be, the same in every respect. Friendship allows for difference, and sometimes—often—it's the very difference that makes the friendship so pleasurable.

And of no one else is it as true as it is of our friends, that we rejoice in their joys, that we are glad for their successes, that we want them to have all the admiration and all the glory due them for their achievements. Their success is our success, even when what they have achieved is something we could never do, and perhaps would never even want to do. 'I'm glad for you', we say, and, when we mean it, that's as close as we get in human relationships to what worship is all about: giving what is God's to God; rejoicing in God and praising God for God's sake.

To speak of God, in Christ, as our friend does not necessarily strip religion of that element of difference that is integral to the spirit of worship. Perhaps, on the contrary, it's only when we realize how near God is, that we are really able to see how different God is, and only when we are with God

24

in the spirit of friendship that we are able to rejoice and be glad in God without reservations.

But perhaps there is also a worry that unless we insist on God's power over us and our duty of obedience, we'll never be sufficiently motivated really to change our lives for the better, really to start living like those who seek to give God what is God's. Being as we are, we humans need to have the whip cracked now and again. We need a God to respect, not a God to be chummy with. Yet this anxiety seems misplaced. After all, human experience shows that we are, on the whole, more likely to do more and to do it better for our friends than for our leaders, managers, or teachers, perhaps even more than for our country. Study after study—and any war film you've ever seen—shows that despite their undoubted loyalty to their Queen, President or country, the primary loyalty of any group of service men and women in action is to their friends. If a soldier performs over and above the call of duty to the point of utter self-sacrifice, nine times out of ten it is for his or her friends. And the reason is obvious to anyone who has any experience of friendship: although friendships sometimes have to be worked at, and although friendships may sometimes seem too good to be believed, our friends' needs are as real to us as our own. As John Henry Newman said, 'Our first life is in ourselves, our second is in our friends.' Our friends are our other lives.

The relation to the superior, to the ruler, to the firm, to the nation, will always be a relation at one remove. The relation to the friend is as spontaneous as a relation to ourselves, and when our friend asks everything of us, we're ready to give it—and we probably do give it, without even thinking that we're doing something especially good or moral or virtuous. We do it just because our friend asked us. To know God in Christ as our friend is not to empty this relationship of its challenge; it is rather to understand it in such a way that we become all the more motivated to do all, to give all, to suffer all, when that's what's asked of us. And as the story of this Last Supper also reminds us, there is no betrayal so great, no pain of being betrayed so great, as when we are betrayed by a friend.

And, lastly, to live with God as a friend is to live with God humbly. Perhaps this is really why the first, and many subsequent, disciples have been hesitant to see their Christian lives as friendship with God. James and John wanted to sit at Christ's right and at his left in his Kingdom, to be his Vice-regents. Paul hints that Peter fancied his role as the first of the apostles. Apostles, it seems, like the idea of sitting on thrones and judging Israel—but such pretensions have no place in friendship. Friendship with God means talking with God about the humble, everyday things you talk about with your friends: your life, your loves, your family, your clothes, your job, the weather. Far from encouraging us to think of ourselves 'as gods', thinking of ourselves as friends of God is the surest way to keep our Christian feet on the ground of humble, everyday reality.

Remembering the Last Supper, as we do tonight, we move from the public arena of the Temple to the intimacy of a private dinner, and from the public offices of prophecy and teaching to the intimacy of a circle of friends. And, just as prophecy and teaching each hold up a mirror in which we are challenged to see ourselves, our hopes and our desires for what they really are; so, too, the company of friends, the circle of our other selves, focuses that same mirror more sharply, because more intimately, and gives us to see—perhaps more clearly than we might like—what we really value, what (and who) really moves us. To claim God as our friend is not impiously to make ourselves 'as gods'; it is to let God be as he wants to be, do for us what he wants to do for us, be there for us in the way he wants to be—that, seeing ourselves as we are in the mirror of his friendship, we might wish to become more as he is, among us as servant… and as friend.

6.

BETRAYAL

'In the night in which he was betrayed ...'[23]

'LET THE CIRCLE BE UNBROKEN' goes the song. But the circle was broken. The circle of friendship was fragmented. The circle gathered to share bread and wine was shattered. The circle of love embracing divine and human—'As you, Father are in me, and I in you, may they also be one in us'—was broken, utterly broken; and Jesus, the centre and unifying force, went out into the night, the night in which he was betrayed.

Jerusalem slept—or, more likely, ate, drank, and talked; the way people eat, drink, and talk in the build-up to any great festival anywhere. Perhaps some talked about the prophet from Galilee—and his presence might have added a little extra excitement to the buzz of anticipation—but, apart from the few score of those directly involved in the events recorded in the gospels, most in Jerusalem probably experienced it as a night like any other night before a major festival. Yet that night, in which they ate, drank, talked and slept, has gone down in history as one of humanity's darkest, as 'the night in which he was betrayed'; or, as he himself said, the 'hour of darkness', the night in which the Prince of this World would show his power to the utmost, striking the shepherd, scattering the flock, turning each against each and all against all, engendering a spiralling vortex of betrayal, denial, and panic. Nor was this a night that would end with sunrise; on the contrary, as the sun rose towards its zenith, the darkness seemed only to deepen until, as the Cross was raised on Golgotha, it became darkness visible: as he who

---

[23] I Cor. 11: 23.

was the Light of the World was raised high on a hilltop for all to see, darkness covered the land.

I am, in principle, a supporter of having our liturgies in contemporary language, but it is hard to deny that there are occasions where something rather important has been lost in the process of revision and updating. One recent Eucharistic prayer has replaced the words, 'On the night in which he was betrayed ...' with, 'On the night before he died ...' This latter describes merely in terms of chronology the night about which we are thinking; and of course it is entirely true that, chronologically, it was on the night before he died that Jesus said and did these things. But 'On the night in which he was betrayed ...' says something more and something different. It says something about the meaning of this night, and why we still remember it, as we do day by day, week by week, in our Eucharistic life.

The prospect of death—whether our own death or the deaths of those we love—is a fearful thing, an inescapable shadow over all human life. But the fearfulness of death is vastly, even qualitatively, magnified if it is no longer a matter of a natural death in the fullness of time, but of a death brought about by human malice. And of all the forms that human malice can take, there is none that hurts so deeply as betrayal. Even when the outcome is not deadly; even when the result of betrayal is merely financial, or social, or a broken heart, the fact that it is the result of a betrayal infinitely compounds whatever loss or pain we are experiencing. We must all die, and, if we are conscious, we will all say or do something on the night before we die. What we say and do will, naturally, be especially remembered by those who are with us, even if it is the most ordinary and everyday word or deed. The imminence of death cannot but add significance to every last detail of such a scene. But it is something else again, if the death we are about to suffer is the result of a betrayal, and above all if it is the result of being betrayed by one whom we had regarded and loved as a friend.

Sometimes it is said that the physical sufferings of the Cross were as nothing compared with the spiritual suffering of the whole Passion. Perhaps those who have experience of comparable physical torture might dare to say such a thing; I cannot. Yet even to one who has never faced anything like the horror of crucifixion, it is clear that the physical agony or the prospect of the physical agony will have been made worse by the knowledge of being betrayed by a friend. We think of the psalmist, when, after lamenting how his enemies maliciously whisper against him, he reaches a climax of misery in the cry that even 'my own familiar friend, in whom I trusted, which did eat of my bread, has lifted up his heel against me'. [24] It is undoubtedly unpleasant—horrific, even— to be spoken against, slandered, attacked, or in any other way to become a victim of human malice. But perhaps we might expect it from enemies, from those who, in some way or other, are 'on the other side' of this or that dispute. But how much worse it is, when the one who does it is 'my own familiar friend, in whom I trusted'.

And yet we might ask: what exactly is the 'extra' involved in betrayal; what is it that makes the suffering so much the worse? Is it simply the thought that if *he* or *she* has betrayed me, then I'm well and truly on my own and there's no one I can trust from now on? Indeed, betrayal weakens or even destroys the basic social trust that makes common human life possible. If we cannot trust our friends, then the world is indeed on the precipice of a war of all against all. Perhaps there has never been a more graphic portrayal of what such a world would be like than the story that progresses from the arrest, through the trials, the beatings, the torture, the mockery, the three crosses on the terrible hillside: this is

---

[24] Ps. 41: 9 (Authorized Version).

humanity in the hour of total mistrust. Each is opposed to all, all are opposed to each, each is on his own, and every man is for himself and himself alone.

Such total and reciprocal mistrust does not stop at our external social relations, however. Its corrosive force penetrates even into the individual's self-relationship, setting a question mark against the very possibility of self-affirmation and self-esteem that, in turn, are basic to individual flourishing.

To see how this is so, let us go back a step. To be attacked, verbally or physically, by an 'enemy', by someone on 'the other side', belongs, in a sense, to the order of the world. There is not much I can do about it, other than seeking to turn enmity into friendship, to become reconciled with those who hate me, with or without a cause. But when I am attacked, openly or covertly, by my friend, I am confronted by a question that does not arise in the case of the enemy. For I have to ask myself whether I myself may not have been guilty of making my friend betray me, of making my friend cease to be my friend and become my enemy. What did I do; what did I say; what did I fail to do; what did I fail to say, that could have had the effect of turning friendship into enmity?

We have several times considered how Jesus's actions, prophecy, and teaching invite us to seek or to deepen self-knowledge, to enquire within as to what it is we really want and what we are really seeking in our lives. But betrayal, too, is an invitation—perhaps the most urgent of all such invitations—to self-scrutiny. And the truer it is that the betrayer is also a friend, the keener such self-scrutiny must be. Even for Jesus, the prospect of betrayal, the possibility that friends could be made into betrayers, must have led to a shattering reflection on the scope and purpose of his mission. For if he came to save—however we understand that—how could it be that his words and actions provoked such a transformation of friendship's sacred bonds? How could he have allowed his friend to become his betrayer? The twentieth century was rather fascinated by the figure of Judas, not least in novels and films of the life of Christ, but the questions we are considering here are not answered by the kinds of speculations that story-tellers are so ingenious in coming up with. For whatever the more precise details of what happened and why, the basic issue of betrayal is not settled by the single case of Judas, since the issue is also implicitly present in the stories of the lesser betrayals, denials and desertions by the other disciples. If there was ever any moment of self-doubt in Jesus's life—and there is nothing in theology that requires us to deny such moments—it was more likely to have been when faced with the realization that he was about to be betrayed, than in the temptation in the wilderness or the confrontations with Scribes and Pharisees.

In the chapter 'The Grand Inquisitor' in his novel *The Brothers Karamazov*, Dostoevsky depicts Jesus returning to sixteenth-century Spain and being apprehended by the Grand Inquisitor, who is in the process of carrying out a particularly spectacular *auto-da-fé*. The Inquisitor rebukes him for refusing the temptation to turn stones into bread, and chides him for overestimating the capacities of human beings. 'You expected from them a freedom of which they are incapable', the Inquisitor says. 'Human beings need earthly bread and earthly rewards to motivate them; they will not follow simply for freedom's sake—but you wouldn't have them, unless they came freely.'[25]

Had Jesus simply asked too much? Had he asked of the disciples a level of freedom and responsibility of which none, or only the few, are really capable? And, in setting his expectations so high, had he himself provoked the betrayal, the flight, the denial that followed? Was it in a sense really his fault?

---

[25] *The Brothers Karamazov*, Fyodor Dostoevsky, Book V, Chapter V.

Dostoevsky's Christ remains silent in the face of the Inquisitor's charge. His only response is to kiss the Inquisitor's bloodless lips. Having asked the question, Dostoevsky was too great a writer and too humble a Christian to pretend to answer it. But, however we might formulate the issue, can we imagine Christ as being human, yet not asking himself such a question, and most urgently, most searingly, in the hour of betrayal? Is the anguish in Gethsemane really understandable if it were only fear for his own life, not also a dread that he had led his friends beyond what they would be capable of bearing? Could he have been satisfied with the explanation that Judas was the 'son of perdition', destined to walk the path of damnation? And could he have experienced each subsequent betrayal, each desertion, each violent blow, each mocking laugh, merely as an expression of the malice of others? Must he not have asked himself whether he hadn't demanded too much, or demanded the wrong things, of them all; setting them tasks, raising expectations that could never be fulfilled? If an experienced mountaineer takes a novice on an exceptionally challenging climb and the novice loses his footing, then it is clearly the novice's mistake, but most would agree that it is the more experienced climber's fault.

The circle of friendship is broken. He goes out into the night, the night in which he was betrayed. It is the hour of darkness, and darkness covers the land. What light can shine in such a darkness? What power can redeem the malice of betrayal, and what answer can be given to the one who has experienced such betrayal? Perhaps there is only one answer, and it is scarcely an answer, only a prayer, the most memorable and the most decisive of the recorded words from the Cross: 'Father, forgive them, for they know not what they do.' For the betrayer rarely thinks of it as a betrayal, but as serving a cause, or doing what must be done, what is 'necessary'. The one who flees and the one who denies does

32

so because there is no choice. Only the one betrayed really experiences the truth that this is indeed a betrayal, the destruction of friendship's intimate bonds of trust. And only such a prayer, by such a betrayed one, can reconcile the betrayer and undo the betrayal.

7.

BURIED

'They saw ... how his body was laid.'[26]

IN THESE TALKS, I have spoken of Jesus's ministry of prophecy and teaching in the public space of the Temple, and of the more intimate conversation he enjoyed with those he called his friends. We now come to a scene that is, in a way, more intimate still: the preparation of the body for burial, and its interment.

One of the great windows in King's College Chapel in Cambridge depicts the three women mentioned in the gospel gathered at the tomb. Holding their spices and ointments, they look down into what is depicted as a stone box tomb of the kind popular in English country churchyards in the eighteenth century. They themselves are portrayed like figures from classical art, one of the women being crowned with a peculiarly spectacular headdress. They are motionless, solemn and dignified in their mourning, their sorrow all the more eloquent for being understated. They seem to be looking into nothingness.

Many of us will have had the experience of standing by the open coffin of a loved one—looking down at what we call the 'body' of someone we have loved, someone who was once alive and laughed and talked and ate and drank, someone we once held in our arms and kissed and hugged—now, nothing, only a 'body' in which there is no sign, not even a flicker, of thought or feeling; only a 'body' in which there is not a trace of human warmth or expression. And if we weep or shout or cry, it makes no difference. There is no response. No response at all. Nothing. The body is lying there, as real as life. But the

---

[26] Luke 23: 55.

34

person we loved is gone, gone so far away that there seems scarcely a link with the body that once was that person. The distance between us has become an infinite distance—literally infinite, for there is no limit, no boundary, no end, to the separation that divides us. 'Between you and us a great chasm has been fixed ...'[27] Nothing we can say, nothing we can do, nothing we can imagine, can bridge that gap. It is too late for 'sorry', too late for 'goodbye', too late for any words. Every bereavement, every sorrow, every loss is, each in its own way, truly infinite.

The image of the three Marys at the tomb shows that moment on Easter morning when the three women (rather differently named in different gospels) arrive at the tomb to anoint the body. As they look down into the tomb, they are then literally looking down into nothingness. There is no body. There is no one there. This is not yet good news, but only a further level of perplexity and grief, believing, as they seem to have done, that the body has been stolen. Yet the picture hints at another truth: that there is a sense in which every coffin, every tomb, is already empty, empty of the person we once loved, empty of the life that filled them, empty of the living being they were. In that sense, Jesus's tomb was as empty on Good Friday as on Easter morning. Even as they laid him in the tomb, tenderly, caringly, lovingly, they would have seen only the nothingness, only the emptiness. *He* was no longer there.

Several times in these talks I have spoken of hope. On Palm Sunday, the arrival in Jerusalem seemed like a living sign of promises fulfilled, an affirmation that the promise of God's kingdom would soon be accomplished. And for all who saw in the mirror of Christ's word an opportunity to learn something new, to become someone new, to become a friend of God, there was much to hope for. And if we also

---

[27] Luke 16: 26.

believe that at a very basic level we are our hopes, if what we hope for defines who we really are, then nothing can be more important than the hope that is in us. Yet whether we think specifically of Christ's death on the Cross, whether we think of the deaths of those near and dear to us, or whether we contemplate our own death, death seems to be the end of hope. Nothingness, emptiness, infinite loss: loss of everything that makes up life: nothing to hope for in the face of *that*.

When Jesus cried on the Cross, 'My God, my God why have you forsaken me?' he knew himself to be falling into this infinite emptiness. He knew he was being snatched away into nothingness, torn out of life and infinitely removed from all who had loved him. There is perhaps no other religion that has at its centre, as its very sign and symbol, such a picture of infinite loss—'dereliction' in the language of the older religious manuals. Such infinity of loss is almost impossible for us to imagine or to conceive, and perhaps it is only in the briefest and sharpest moments of grief that we even glimpse it. Yet we know that, unless or until we have reckoned with it, we are only beginners in the mysteries of God. Several times in these talks I have used the image of a mirror, thinking of Christ's words of prophecy and teaching as a mirror in which we see ourselves, our wants, our hearts, magnified and clarified. But what if the truest mirror of all is this empty tomb, and what if all we see when we look into it is this infinite nothingness, this infinite loss?

To reckon with the infinity of loss, to stare at an image of ourselves as sheer emptiness, nothing at all, not just dead, but gone: how can we do that? It is not just a matter of not being able to picture this, of not having a concept for this. Perhaps in a way we can picture it or conceive of it after all, like the writer who defined the human being as a 'six-foot nothing'; but these pictures and concepts just don't engage the reality. There is no proportion of scale, no measure we can use, to bring our pictures or concepts into any kind of relation to such an infinity. They may not be wrong, but they are on the wrong scale—like trying to measure the passing of time on our kitchen scales. Maybe there is some analogy between a long day and a heavy weight, but we have no instrument for bringing them into relation to one another. What is 'six foot' cannot be 'nothing', because what is 'nothing' has no height or length or breadth.

What could measure the infinity of loss that is opened up in the grave of Christ, in God's grave, in every grave? What do we have left to steer by, when every hope is gone? 'Faith, hope, and love abide', said Paul.[28] On Palm Sunday I suggested that, for us in our time, hope may be even more fundamental than faith. But perhaps even hope is liable to fail in the face of this nothingness, this emptiness. There is, then, only one word left: love. Even love may not be able to show us what lies on the far side of the infinite loss in which human life ends, but in its way love gives us a measure with which to measure our loss, a plummet that reaches into those infinite depths as far as human hearts can reach. Love measures and sets the only possible limit to this otherwise immeasurable infinity.

In the deaths of others, we lose those we love, and we see something of our own coming death, in which we will lose life itself and fall into that infinite emptiness. In the death of Jesus, those who loved him, his friends—we too, if we are his friends—see the death of one who was the very image of God's love, of one who said of himself 'I am Life'. No loss could be more complete. Love gone, life gone, nothing remains. Yet even here at the empty tomb—and empty even in the moment he was laid in it—there is, after all, love. He was love, and those who have followed him to this empty tomb remain in that love. And in that love, they have a measure with which to set a limit to the infinity of their loss, a

---

[28] I Cor. 13: 13.

new name with which to baptize that nothing which each of us is: the new, best name of love.

In that moment at the tomb, staring down into the infinite distance which death has set between us and him, we learn that our last possibility, beyond belief, beyond hope, is the possibility of love. Love alone names the nothingness that each of us must become. Our best hope must surely be, in time, to be so named, that love may follow us to our final resting place. For only in love and by love is Jesus named our Saviour, Redeemer, Friend; only in love and by love is his death named our Salvation.

8.

EASTER

'He is going ahead of you to Galilee, there you will see him.'[29]

IN ST MATTHEW'S GOSPEL, when the women arrive at the tomb, they are met by an angel who instructs them to give the following message to the other disciples:

> He has been raised from the dead, and indeed he is going ahead of you to Galilee; there you will see him.[30]

> He is going ahead of you to Galilee, there you will see him.[31]

Galilee, the place where it all began; the place where Jesus himself grew up; where, walking by the lakeside, he first called Peter and the others to become his followers. Galilee, whose towns and villages, no more significant in themselves than the towns and villages of Oxfordshire, have become household names around the world: Nazareth, Capernaum, Cana, Gennesaret, where Jesus gave his teaching, worked miracles, and prophetically acted to break the social barriers raised against lepers, tax gatherers, fallen women, and religious and ethnic outsiders. Galilee, the place from which they themselves had come, where they had grown up, plied their trade, in some cases married, maybe had children. Until, that was, *he* appeared and led them off along wilderness tracks, up mountains, to the coasts of Tyre and through the strange country of the Samaritans, and so down to the great, rich, violent city of Jerusalem, where they themselves would experience deep social and religious prejudice against

---

[29] Matt. 28: 7; Mark 16: 7.
[30] Matt. 28: 7.
[31] Mark 16: 7.

provincial outsiders such as themselves, and where, finally (or so it seemed) he had been seized, tortured, and executed.

Galilee would always be for them a place of memories, childhood memories (usually the best), memories of young adulthood, of the comradeship of work, of family festivities where they ate and drank and danced till dawn, and, for some of them (probably) memories of first love. A place where they had faced some dangers—life was never without dangers in the ancient world—learned hard lessons, faced setbacks. A place which was *home,* where they were from, their background. A place which meant familiarity, security, identity; a place where they knew their place in the positive sense of knowing who they were and where they stood and how to deal with the people and situations they encountered. A place which was *home,* as it has been for anyone, anywhere, at any time in history, and as it has been for each of us, wherever we were born and grew up.

And it was there, in their home country, that he had met them and called them, turned their world upside down, given them new ideas, taken them to new places, led them into strange and unfamiliar situations and confronted them with physical dangers and moral challenges they'd never reckoned with before. And now the adventure was over. He was dead. That chapter of their lives was closed: time to pack up and go home; a painful moment. Not least because of the horror of his death. Not least because the whole thing had ended in failure. Not least because that failure was compounded by a burning sense of their own inadequate response to it, a response some would call a cowardly betrayal—and, probably, being young men, they would feel that charge more keenly than any. Yet, there was home, somewhere to go back to, somewhere familiar, a place in the world where they could pick up the threads and, despite it all, be someone again. However bitter the circumstances, there is always some comfort in returning home.

The pattern is not unfamiliar: indeed, it is already there in the earliest great works of Western literature—Homer's two great poems, the *Iliad* and the *Odyssey*. Even today these works are never out of print. Amazon can offer you literally dozens of alternative translations. They are told for children, adapted for radio, filmed (usually disastrously), and constantly retranslated. Why do they touch us so deeply? Of course, the poetry has a lot to do with it, but even the simplest outline of the story of these two great books gives us another clue. The first tells the story of the Greek forces setting out to wage war on the distant shores of Asiatic Troy. The second tells the story of how one of the Greeks, Odysseus, made the long and tortuous journey home, back to the faithful wife and the familiar house he'd left those many years before. The journey out into the world; and the journey home. How much of our experience can be compressed into these few words! We all need to get out, to go somewhere, to do something, to have something that, in however modest a way, we can call an adventure. And we all need home, somewhere to go back to, somewhere where there will be people to hear about our adventures and, if necessary, patch up our wounds.

Is this, then, the disciples' story? Is this the Christian story?

Not exactly… Yes, they are to go home, to return to Galilee, to go back to where it all started—and that's where we see them in today's gospel, breakfasting by the lakeside, as before. Peter has been reunited with his wife, like Odysseus with Penelope. Boats have been kitted out, and perhaps Matthew will re-open his ledger books. Familiarity will return, and the three years on the road become a memory—and although they will be a painful memory at first, perhaps in time it'll be good to relive those memories by the fireside or walking out on the hillsides, the way old

41

soldiers get some comfort from returning to battlefields that, when they were battlefields, were hell on earth.

Yes, they are to go home, to return to Galilee. But not to the lives they'd lived before. Not to what they thought they knew. Not to sit and remember the man they thought they'd known. It seems there's one more trick in the book; one more surprise card. They are to go home—but not to home as they knew it. They are not leaving him behind in Jerusalem. They are not leaving their life with him behind in Jerusalem. He is going before them to Galilee. And, as he joins them for breakfast, they know that he is not just a part of their past. He is, and always will be (it seems) a part of their future. The one they don't yet entirely know. The one they still have to discover. The one who will always be going before them: to Galilee and then—as we know—beyond Galilee to Greece, to Rome, to the ends of the earth.

On Easter morning, the gospels tell us, there was a lot of running: the women running from the tomb, Peter and the disciple whom Jesus loved running to the tomb. And, from now on, they're going to be running for the rest of their lives, running to catch up with the one who is, who will always be, going on before them. The story is not finished with the return home. It is about to begin. Home will and can never be what it was. They—and Christians ever since—have become just a little bit dislocated, strangers and pilgrims in the world, travellers who doubtless love their homes and all that belongs to home, but who are also haunted by the memory—or is it the anticipation?—of another country, another place, another kind of home, a home that all of us somehow know, yet a home where none of us has ever quite been, a promised land still to find.

Running after him, straining to catch up with the man they thought they'd known, not entirely knowing where he is leading them, the disciples learn two things about the Christian life, the Christian spirit—and so can we. Because the promised land is still for us to find, because we do not yet know what, in following him, we still have to learn, or what, in following him, we still have to *become*, our lives will be marked from top to bottom and from start to finish by the expectation of something new to be learned, something new about to happen, some adventure still to be lived. That is one half of the Christian spirit. Yet, because *he* is going before us, this is not quite the same as the 'adventures' of those who first go out into the world not knowing what is going to happen to them or where or why they are going. Disciples, homeless voyagers as they have become, know that they don't know all there is to know about him, and they never will. But they do know what they have experienced with him; they do know something of what the promise of his presence amongst them means; and they look to the future, not only with hope, but also with confidence. And, although they know only in part,[32] they do, in part, know whom they have believed and trusted. Because there is, and always will be, one going before them, their journey is with a purpose, and there is a confidence in their stride. And that is the other half of the Christian spirit. 'Behold, he is going before you to Galilee'—to the home that is no longer home in the way it once was—there you will see him; and where he is leading you, that is really home.

---

[32] I Cor. 13: 9.